The Art of the Scarf

From classic knots and
chic neckties, to stylish turbans,
makeshift bags and more

Illustrated by
Libby VanderPloeg

hardie grant books

Contents

Introduction

A deftly tied scarf can take any outfit from basic to brilliant and transform the simple to the sublime. This book contains 30 tutorials to up your scarf game without tying yourself in knots.

You'll find plenty of neck-scarf tutorials, from the classic Loop (page 12) to the elegant Rose (page 42). But the scarf can be so much more – a bag (page 34), a belt (pages 44 and 72) or even a halter-top (page 16). Turn scarves from winter warmer to summer staple with beach-ready outfits such as the Sarong (page 24) and the Dress (page 46).

Try out new trends without breaking the bank with fashion-forward looks like the edgy Cape (page 54) or inventive Bracelet (page 82). And make bad-hair days an opportunity to work the statement Turban (page 52) or pretty Halo (page 74).

Take inspiration from style icons such as Frida Kahlo, Jackie O and Kate Moss, learn about the history of scarves and their designers, and create your own signature look. Master the art of the scarf!

Types of Scarf

Blanket Scarf

A large blanket scarf can help you stay cosy in winter, but also be used for dramatic statement outfits.

Infinity Scarf

The infinity scarf is joined at both ends and is a quick shortcut to achieving intricate loops.

Ribbon Scarf

Versatile ribbon scarves can
be used as neckties, bracelets
and hair ribbons.

Rectangular Scarf

Often in wool or thicker fabrics, the
rectangular scarf is excellent for
neck-scarf looks.

Square Scarf

The classic scarf shape, which can be
folded to achieve almost any look.
Choose silk for a luxurious touch.

History of the Scarf

The scarf was one of the first pieces of clothing to be invented – from the ancient Egyptians to the Romans, people have been draping scarves around themselves since the concept of fashion came into being. The scarf transcends trends and crosses cultures.

Nefertari, the wife of Pharoah Ramses II, was the first fierce queen to wear a scarf – her ornate headdress sat atop a gorgeous head wrap. To steal her regal style with a modern twist, try the Head Wrap on page 90.

The ancient Greeks wore whole outfits composed of artfully pinned scarves, along with shawls and hair ribbons, while Roman women wore long scarves over their tunics. Although stepping out in a toga might get you some stares, there's nothing stopping you from turning your scarves into full-blown outfits. Make your scarves do double-duty with the Dress on page 46 or the Playsuit on page 78.

Marie Antoinette famously spent more time thinking about her accessories than her subjects. She and other Rococo ladies decorated their elaborate wigs with powder, feathers, ribbons and of course, scarves. Try out the contemporary take on her Turban (page 52).

The sensual silk scarf is sure to win you admirers – just ask Beethoven, who cultivated a style focused around dandyish scarves in a bid to attract Therese Malfatti. Copy his look with the Boy Scout on page 22 or the Tie on page 88.

The 20th century was an explosion of opportunity for scarf style, and now there are more options than ever. Turn to the Scarf Directory on page 94 to discover a list of the best scarf designers and shops, and take inspiration throughout from some of the best known scarf icons.

The Loop

Relaxed, understated,
effortless – this simple knot
will transform any outfit.

1. Drape the scarf around your neck.

2. Loop the scarf around your neck, making sure both ends are of equal length.

3. Tie a knot with the loose ends of the scarf.

4. Arrange the loose circle over the knot and bask in casual chic.

1. Use a rectangular scarf or fold a square scarf into a rectangle. Loop the scarf around the back of your head and take both ends around to your forehead, pulling tight.

2. At the top of your head, take one end of the scarf under the other end of the scarf, pulling tight.

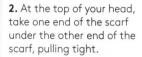

3. Secure with a knot.

4. Tuck the loose ends under the headband you have created and enjoy the finished look. Red lipstick and raised eyebrow optional.

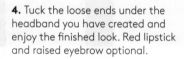

The Riveter

Inspired by wartime hero Rosie the Riveter, this daring headscarf is easy to achieve and will add a fashionista twist to your look.

The Halter Top

Look and feel cool
in summer with a
relaxed halter.

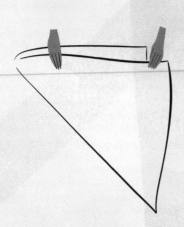

1. Fold a large square scarf diagonally in half to form a triangle.

2. With the point of the triangle facing down, take the other two corners back around your neck.

3. Secure with a knot at the nape of your neck.

4. Pull the loose edges of your scarf back around your torso and secure with a knot at the back. Get out and enjoy the breeze.

SCARF ICON

Greta Garbo

Greta Garbo (1905–1990) remembered her childhood in Stockholm as "eternally grey" and set about to transform her adult life into anything but. The Swedish actor – and onetime model – made her name in European cinema before moving to the US in 1925 at the bequest of MGM studios' Louis B. Mayer. There, she learned English, refined her look with yoga and pilates, and in 1930 appeared in a string of silent movies before undertaking her first speaking role in *Anna Christie* (her first line, delivered in a boozy drawl, was "Gimme a whiskey, ginger ale on the side, and don't be stingy, baby.")

> *"Perhaps I am most pleased at having fought for the right for women to wear trousers."*
>
> **GRETA GARBO**

Garbo's personal style balanced refined Hollywood elegance with a steadfast European practicality. Official studio portraits show her in furs, diamonds, and a bejewelled turban, but her off duty outfits were more androgynous: she favoured the designer Valentina Schlee, and styled shirts and lounge pants with a scarf, flat shoes, and a simple string of pearls. Later, as her fame grew – as much the result of her fame as an actor as her rumoured liaisons with men and women – she added more scarves to her repertoire along with black straw hats and dark glasses as she hid from the paparazzi until she retired from show business altogether.

1. Take the scarf around the nape of your neck and cross both ends over at your forehead.

2. Fold both ends in half around each other.

3. Pull tightly and secure in a knot at the nape of your neck. Tuck the loose ends under.

The Headband

Geek chic never
looked so good.

The Boy Scout

A classic look, loved by Boy Scouts and glamorous air hostesses alike. Be prepared!

1. Fold the scarf diagonally into a triangle, roll up and drape around your neck.

2. Loop the scarf around your neck.

3. Pull one end of the scarf through the loop.

4. Tie both ends of the scarf into a small knot and ensure the knot is kept hidden.

The Sarong

The perfect outfit for lazy days and moonlit beach strolls.

1. Hold either end of a large scarf out around your back.

2. Take both ends of the scarf around to your front, cross over your shoulders, secure at the nape of your neck with a knot and ensure the scarf drapes beautifully over your body.

SCARF ICON

Grace Kelly

Like a living, breathing Disney character, Grace Kelly (1929–1982) was the movie star, style icon, and real-life Princess of Monaco; the upper-class beauty who married a prince and lived happily ever after with 101 scarves at her disposal (probably). Kelly attended the American Academy of Dramatic Arts in New York and played minor roles on Broadway until she scored the lead role in a TV drama, performing almost 60 live shows. Then, she set about breaking Hollywood in classics like *High Society* and Alfred Hitchcock's *Dial M For Murder*, *Rear Window*, and *To Catch a Thief*.

> *"I believe that it is right to honour all those who create beautiful things and give satisfaction to those who see me wearing them."*
>
> **GRACE KELLY**

Kelly was undeniably an icon of style (and scarves), the studios – and her fans – loved her wholesome, all-American look with its dash of easy elegance and glamour. In 1955, at a photo op for *Paris Match* magazine in Cannes, Kelly met Prince Rainier III of Monaco and the pair married a year later. For the two wedding ceremonies – meticulously photographed and watched by 30 million people across the world on live TV – she wore a dress by her MGM costume designer Helen Rose. A year after her marriage, Kelly took her love of Hermès scarves to new heights when she used one of their silk scarves as a sling for her broken arm. Although Kelly later retired from acting, she remained a firm fixture in celebrity magazines; a true princess of style.

The Baboushka

Turn unruly hair into
a stylish statement.

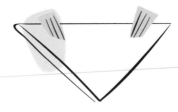

1. Tie your hair in a low bun, then fold your scarf diagonally to create a triangle.

2. Grasping opposite corners, drape the triangle over your head to cover your hair. Make sure the long side is across your forehead and the point of the triangle hangs down over the nape of your neck.

3. Bring the corners of the scarf down and cross over underneath your bun.

4. Take the corners up to the top of your bun and tie the scarf into a small knot.

5. Tie the corners of the scarf underneath the bun, tucking any loose ends away.

1. Drape a rectangular scarf around your neck.

2. Cross one end over the other.

3. Cross the ends over one more time and bring them around to the back of your neck.

4. Secure with a knot.

The Choker

Spruce up a simple T-shirt
with the addition of an
effortlessly chic choker.

Sophia Loren

Sophia Loren is the Oscar-winning Italian actress who – in her 1960s heyday – starred in movie classics like *The Pride and the Passion* and *It Started in Naples*. She commanded a million-dollar fee for *The Fall of the Roman Empire*, and performed an on-screen striptease in 1963's *Yesterday, Today, and Tomorrow*. Not bad for a runner-up in the Miss Italia beauty contest, 1950. Although the press has long been preoccupied with Loren's steamy sex-symbol status, she has in fact underlined her prolific career with jaw-dropping performances, from Vittorio de Sica's *Two Women* (1961) to Ettore Scola's *A Special Day* (1977).

"I look fantastic. Everybody says so!"

SOPHIA LOREN

One of the most popular actresses of her day, Loren's unique off-camera style – glamourous and unabashedly sexual – has secured her place as a true legend of style. Along with her glasses (she loves a pair of specs), dramatic eye make-up and trademark pale pink lipstick, her love of scarves has endured. Sophia has spent the last few years with her family, appearing in a small selection of handpicked films, and flipped a middle finger to ageism by appearing lingerie-clad in the Pirelli calendar at the age of 71.

1. Spread out a large square scarf.

2. Knot together
two opposite corners.

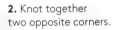

3. Raise the loose corners
to form a bag shape.

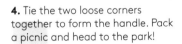

4. Tie the two loose corners
together to form the handle. Pack
a picnic and head to the park!

The Bag

Utility and style in perfect harmony.

1. Tie your hair into a low bun or ponytail.

2. Take a ribbon scarf or a small scarf folded into a slim rectangle. Wrap it around your bun and secure with a knot at the top.

3. Tie the loose ends of the scarf into a pretty bow.

The Hair Ribbon

Give your ponytail or plait a 50s feel with a playful ribbon.

SCARF ICON

Audrey Hepburn

There are few characters in cinema as iconic than Audrey Hepburn's Holly Golightly in the big-screen adaptation of Truman Capote's *Breakfast at Tiffany's*. The young ingénue, all spindle limbs and towering bouffant hair in a Givenchy column dress, is considered one of Hepburn's most captivating characters with a wardrobe of iconic outfits that are timelessly cool – not least her Burberry trench coat and head scarf at the end of the film.

> "When I wear a silk scarf I never feel so definitely like a woman. a beautiful woman."
>
> **AUDREY HEPBURN**

Hepburn was born in Brussels and spent her childhood between the UK, Belgium and the Netherlands, learning ballet in German-occupied Arnhem in WWII before moving to London in 1948 to perform as a chorus girl in West End productions. She appeared in a few films and the Broadway production of *Gigi* before scoring the neckerchief-loving lead in *Roman Holiday* (1953), and scooped up an Oscar, BAFTA and Golden Globe for her efforts. Known for her refined, chic approach to style, Hepburn collaborated with designers and costumiers, and travelled to Paris to meet Hubert de Givenchy to source her own clothes for the film *Sabrina* (1954). Hers was a confidently simple look she described as a "spare style" that would hang on the use of a single well-chosen accessory, just a pair of earrings, Tod's Italian shoes – or a scarf, of course.

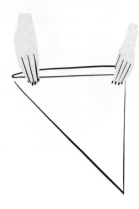

1. Fold a square scarf in half to make a triangle.

2. Drape it over your head, with the folded edge in front.

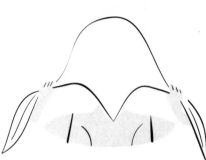

3. Bring the ends of the scarf together under your chin and cross them over.

4. Wrap around your neck, tucking the points of the triangle into the scarf and secure to one side with a loose knot. Grab your shades and hit the road!

The Road Trip

Channel your inner
Hollywood starlet with
this iconic look.

The Rose

Take florals to the next level with an elegant and interesting neck scarf.

1. Use a rectangular scarf or fold a square scarf into a rectangle. Drape around your neck.

2. Twist one end of the scarf around the other until you reach the bottom.

3. Roll the twist into a rose shape.

4. Tuck the loose end of the scarf behind the rose to secure.

1. Fold a scarf into a long, thin rectangle.

2. Tuck the scarf through the belt loops of your favourite skirt or trousers and bring the ends towards the front.

3. Secure to one side with a knot and let the loose ends hang.

The Belt

This updated belt adds
a flash of colour and
texture to any outfit.

The Dress

Make your most beautiful scarves the centre of attention.

1. Wrap a large, rectangular scarf around your back, keeping hold of the corners.

2. Bring the ends around to the front, twisting as you go.

3. Cross each end over the other and secure with a knot at the base of your neck.

SCARF ICON

Frida Kahlo

Born in Mexico City in 1907, Frida Kahlo is the artist, feminist icon, and brave taboo-breaker who had a completely unique artistic and personal style. Kahlo grew up in post-revolution Mexico, contracted polio as a child, survived a bus crash in her teens (that left her with bouts of intense pain for the rest of her life), and had an infamously volatile relationship with fellow artist Diego Rivera. Little wonder that revolution, pain and love were the themes that informed her art.

Creating a number of self-portraits, Kahlo left an important artistic legacy – although for many years after her death she was known simply as Diego Rivera's wife, until her posthumous fame eclipsed his, making her arguably the world's most famous female artist.

> *"I am my own muse.*
> *I am the subject I know best."*
>
> **FRIDA KAHLO**

Kahlo felt a deep connection to clothing and her personal style – blazing with colour and shape – was an integral part of her identity. She rejected the fashion of the day and eschewed delicate flapper frocks for bright embroidered dresses and cats eye glasses, corset tops, and traditional Mexican clothing – with a never-ending range of scarves and accessories. The most iconic images of Kahlo show her with turbans, scarves, and flowers in her hair, in eclectic, anti-fashion, and eye-poppingly gorgeous outfits that still inspire and empower today.

1. Choose a large blanket scarf.

2. Drape around your shoulders. Bring one end of the scarf across your body and tuck it behind your shoulder.

3. Throw the other end of the scarf over the opposite shoulder.

The Understatement

Instantly update your winter
wardrobe with the ultimate
in comfy street style.

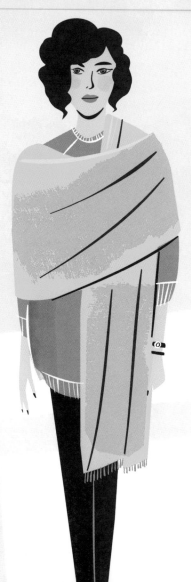

The Turban

Lana Turner made this look
famous in the 1940s classic
The Postman Always Rings Twice,
and now you can too.

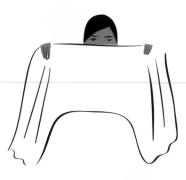

1. Choose a wide rectangular scarf.

2. Lean forward and drape over your head, with the edge of the scarf at the nape of your neck.

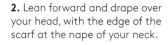

3. Bring the ends together and twist tightly to form a single rope.

4. Twist into a rose at your forehead, tucking the ends under to secure. Use bobby pins to keep in place all day.

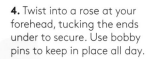

1. Spread out a large square scarf.

2. Bring the top left and bottom left corners together and secure with a small knot. Do the same with the top right and bottom right corners.

3. Slip your arms into the spaces you have created. Take on the world.

The Cape

Looking super has never
been easier.

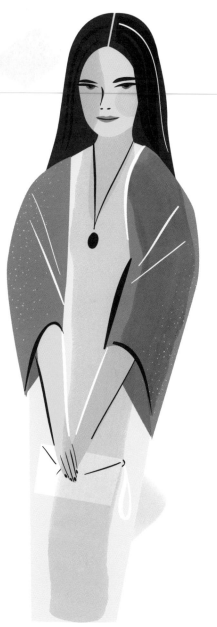

SCARF ICON

Jackie O

If the USA has anything like an unofficial royal family, it's the Kennedys, and Jacqueline Lee Kennedy (1929–1994) was its Chanel-suited queen. As a young woman, the horse-loving East Hampton socialite's parents instilled in her an unshakable confidence; she studied French Literature at John Washington, won a junior editorship at *Vogue* (a position she left after one day), and in 1953 she went on to marry the catch of the century, successful playboy with a social conscience, congressman John F. Kennedy. By the time JFK became president in 1961, Jackie was already a something of a trendsetter in the press, but her time in the White House made her a fashion icon.

> ## "*I am a woman above everything else.*"
> **JACKIE O**

She was a lover of neck-scarves, little black dresses and sleeveless frocks, pillbox hats and the world's biggest sunglasses. Stepping away from the formalities of political journalism, photographers followed the Kennedys behind the scenes, creating a loose, reportage-style document of their lives and Jackie restored and revamped the White House interiors, in a symbolic gesture that signalled a new age. Following JFK's assassination in 1963 and her marriage to Aristotle Onassis in 1968, Jackie O withdrew from the public eye, which seemed only to underline her celebrity. Then a successful book editor, her scant public appearances became legendary and her popularity and elegant, easy style continue to inspire.

1. Take a long, thin, rectangular scarf or fold a square scarf into a rectangle.

2. Pass the scarf around your neck, under your hair, and bring the ends forward and upwards, behind your ears.

3. Secure with a pretty bow at the top of your head.

The Alice

Transport yourself to Wonderland with this simple but stunning look.

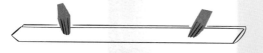

1. Fold each side of your scarf lengthways to meet in the middle. Repeat until you have a narrow rectangle.

2. Tie a knot in the centre of the scarf.

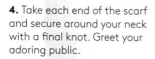

3. Tie two more knots on either side of the first knot, halfway between the ends of the scarf and the centre knot.

4. Take each end of the scarf and secure around your neck with a final knot. Greet your adoring public.

The Necklace

No jewellery? No problem.

SCARF ICON

Erykah Badu

Erykah Badu (1971) is the singer-songwriter, producer, actor, passionate activist, and the award-winning creative behind the albums *Baduizm*, *Mama's Gun*, and *New Amerykah Part One and Two*. She also looks 100 percent amazing in a scarf. Born in Dallas, Texas, Badu burst into popular culture via the iconic *Baduizm* album cover on which she wore a headscarf, intricately arranged, with her face turned away from the camera. Unheard of in today's curated online world, Badu rarely works with a stylist or art director on a look that is peppered with turbans and hair wraps, or an immense cloud of brushed out hair.

> *"Accessories really are everything for me."*
>
> **ERYKAH BADU**

Her strong sense of personal style has lead to collaborations with designers Riccardo Tisci and Tom Ford, and her adventures in menswear see her wear blazers, shirts, and men's trousers, gathered at the waist, or loose workwear overalls. Her sound is at the forefront of neo-soul, drawing in elements of hip hop, R&B and jazz, and her loyal fans see to it that she tours eight months of every year. On the road, Badu always carries with her a huge holdall packed with myriad accessories – silver jewellery and crystals, Maasai beads and space for six hats in her hat box.

The Kahlo

Complete Frida's signature look by pinning large, bright flowers in your hair around your forehead.

1. Part your hair in the centre and tie your hair into two high bunches.

2. Take a ribbon scarf or a scarf folded into a slim rectangle. Pass it diagonally between the bunches.

3. Pass one end of the scarf around one of the bunches and back towards the other bunch.

4. Loop the scarf back around the second bunch to form a figure-of-eight.

5. Divide the first bunch into two. Braid the hair and scarf together, using the scarf like a third strand of hair. Repeat with the second bunch.

6. Secure in a beautiful crown shape using hairpins. Accessorise with bold brow(s).

1. Fold a large blanket scarf into a triangle.

2. Drape the scarf around your shoulders, bringing the corners around to the front of your body.

3. Cross one side over the other and secure with a belt. Stay snug and cosy all day long.

The Blanket Wrap

If you must get out of bed,
why not take your blanket
with you?

SCARF ICON

Kate Moss

Croydon's finest export, Kate Moss (1974) is the party-loving, waif-like model discovered by Storm Models founder Sarah Doukas in 1988, and made famous by the late photographer Corinne Day in her legendary shoot for *The Face* magazine. For more than 25 years, Moss has been at the forefront of international fashion, appearing in countless catwalk shows and ad campaigns, working with the world's best photographers, and enjoying the odd celebrity romance (remember the Johnny Depp years?). In the 90s, Moss was thought of as the anti-supermodel – she was the polar opposite of the impossibly tall, curvaceous Claudia Schiffer, Elle Macpherson and Cindy Crawford, and her skinny looks placed her at the centre of a grungy, minimalist and unpolished look that acquired the (somewhat cruel) title of heroin chic.

> *"I'm not really a fashion designer. I just love clothes... I can make a dress out of a scarf."*
>
> **KATE MOSS**

Since her early years, Moss has radiated a natural, pared-back elegance, and her brand has rarely diminished, surviving dodgy relationships and controversies, making her one of the most successful models ever. Moss's personal style often sees her in a simple yet perfectly put together uniform of skinny jeans, cropped biker jackets and loosely draped scarves from her favourite luxury brands, and she's as much at home on the red carpet or at the Met Gala as she is cavorting around Glastonbury in a pair of mud-splattered wellies.

1. Fold a square scarf into a triangle and place it over your head, point facing down towards your neck.

2. Secure with a knot at the nape of your neck.

The Biker

Vintage glamour
in a flash.

The Braided Belt

Choose similar colours for a subtle look, or be bold with clashing patterns and prints.

1. Select three long, narrow rectangular scarves.

2. Gather the ends.

3. Plait the scarves together in a classic braid, using one hand to keep the top secure.

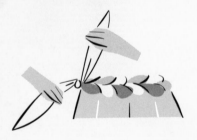

4. Tie around your waist, securing on one side with a knot and leaving the ends loose.

1. Drape a long rectangular scarf over your head.

2. Twist each end of the scarf into two braids.

3. Take one braid over the top of your head and secure at the other side of the neck.

4. Repeat with the other braid in the opposite direction and secure.

The Halo

This braided crown will
have you looking angelic
no matter what you're up to.

SCARF ICON

Brigitte Bardot

Listen to Serge Gainsbourg's 'Initials B.B.' and you'll hear a lush, orchestral pop ode to the French actress, vocalist, model, animal lover, and icon of style, Brigitte Bardot (1934). With her giant, tousled blonde locks and door-stop eyelashes, the scarf-wearing Bardot is so much more than just a muse. Still, her time spent collaborating with the cult French musician in the late 1960s was her heyday and images from this period are perhaps her most iconic. The aspiring ballerina appeared in 16 comedic films from 1952 until 1957, when her celebrity rocketed after appearing in the controversial ... And God Created Woman in a barely-there bikini. She became a figure of interest to Simone de Beauvoir and other French intellectuals who saw her through an existialist lens, and subsequently went on to appear in films by Jean-Luc Goddard and Louis Malle, along with a string of international mega hits and warbly songs.

> *"Fashion may not be a weapon of the woman but at least it gives her the ammunition."*
>
> **BRIGITTE BARDOT**

Her contribution to contemporary style is unquestionable: that loose-fit top that exposes both shoulders? It's known as a Bardot neckline. That messy, sexy version of a beehive? It's another Bardot classic. That cute, gingham dress? Bardot again. Her most iconic photographs show her in any number of cute scarves – knotted bandana style across her forehead or lightly tied over her hair; impossibly chic and very B.B.

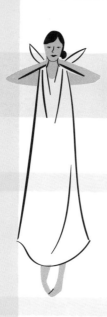

1. Grab the top two corners of a large scarf and secure in a knot at the nape of your neck.

2. Take the loose end of the scarf between your legs and behind your back. Grasp the corners and hold out at either side.

3. Secure the bottom corners in a knot at your navel, followed by a bow. Sunbathe, stroll and eat ice cream in style.

The Playsuit

The beach doesn't have
to be basic.

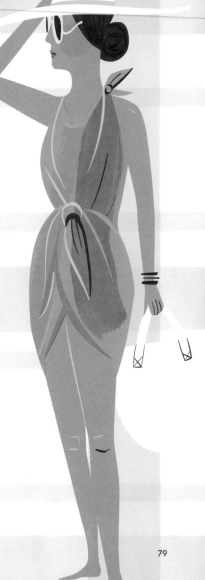

The Jetsetter

Perfect for when you need
to travel in style.

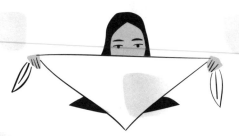

1. Fold a square scarf in half to form a triangle.

2. With the triangle in front, cross the ends of the scarf at the back of your neck and bring forward.

3. Tie the corners together to secure before flying off into the sunset.

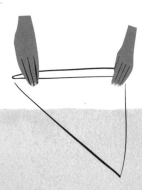

1. If using a square scarf, fold into a triangle.

2. Fold into a slim rectangle.

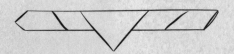

3. Wrap the scarf around your wrist, making the bracelet as thick or thin as you like.

4. Secure with a knot. Wear one on each wrist for maximum impact.

The Bracelet

Wear alone for a simple pop
of colour, or pile up alongside all
the bracelets in your jewellery
box – the choice is yours.

SCARF ICON

Jane Birkin

Could British actor Jane Birkin (1946) be the coolest woman in the world? At the epicenter of London's Swinging Sixties scene, the young actress appeared in cult films *Blowup* and *Wonderwall* before securing a role in France on the film *Slogan* in 1968 (despite not speaking any French) where her co-star was musician Serge Gainsbourg. Thus began a rather fruity history of creative collaboration – their saucy duet *Je t'aime... moi non plus* was banned by radio stations in Italy, Spain, and the UK – and the couple had a child together, Charlotte Gainsbourg. Birkin's cool style made her a fashion icon; in the late 1960s and 70s she was the waifish, enigmatic British It girl with Parisian pretentions.

> *"My mother was right: When you've got nothing left, all you can do is get into silk underwear and start reading Proust."*

JANE BIRKIN

Her effortless, chic sense of style in this period has had an enduring influence. The most arresting photography of Birkin shows her in loose shirting and denim, scuffed white plimsolls, loose scarves and bandanas tied around the wrist. A chance meeting on a flight from Paris to London inspired a fellow passenger, Hermès chief exec Jean-Louis Dumas, to create the Birkin bag (after the actor dropped the contents of her straw bag on the floor). The bag is now the world's most cultish (and expensive) accessory with a rumoured waiting list of years. A little ostentatious for the wonderfully dressed-down style icon, but a testament to Birkin's cool, all the same.

1. Take a long, thin, rectangular scarf or fold a square scarf into a rectangle.

2. Wrap the scarf around your head.

3. Secure with a knot at the side, letting the ends dangle loosely.

The Woodstock

Whether you're powering
through the last day of a festival
or wouldn't go within 10 feet
of a tent, this is your shortcut
to laidback 60s glamour.

1. If using a square scarf, fold into a slim rectangle.

2. Drape the scarf around your neck and under your collar, if wearing.

3. Loop one end of the scarf around the other, bringing it up and over.

4. Cross the same end over the other once more.

5. Bring it up through the loop around your neck.

6. Tuck the end through the knot and pull to adjust and tighten.

The Tie

Take inspiration
from menswear for
effortless cool.

The Head Wrap

This chic wrap keeps your
locks under control.

1. Spread out a large square or rectangular scarf.

2. Drape over your head, bringing the ends forward towards the forehead.

3. Gather the loose ends together at one side of your head.

4. Secure with a knot.

5. Braid the ends of the scarf together and round to the side of your head.

6. Tuck the ends underneath the scarf at the nape of your neck.

Caring for Your Scarves

Your scarves make you look amazing, so it's only fair to keep them looking as great as the day you bought them.

Always follow the washing instructions on the care labels of your scarves. Some scarves, especially vintage silk scarves, are dry-clean only or should not be washed at all. The dyes on hand-painted scarves will run if they are placed in water. Proceed with caution!

Some scarves can be machine-washed, but hand washing is generally best, and doesn't take too much elbow grease. To hand wash scarves, fill a sink with cool water and a few drops of mild detergent. Make sure you use a detergent specially formulated for the material, especially if your scarf is silk. Gently swirl the scarf around in the soapy water, then rinse until all the suds have disappeared. Spread out the wet scarf onto a towel, roll up and squeeze. Never wring out delicate scarves. Iron the scarf dry under a clean handkerchief, avoiding the edges.

The best way to store delicate or valuable scarves is to fold and place in drawers, or store in the box they were bought in. To save space, you may want to hang cheaper or sturdier scarves. Try to keep your scarves out of direct sunlight to avoid their vibrant colours fading.

Scarf Directory

UK

Accessorize

www.accessorize.com

Marks & Spencer

www.marksandspencer.com

AUSTRALIA

Blue Illusion

www.blueillusion.com

David Jones

www.davidjones.com.au

Myer

www.myer.com.au

Sportsgirl

www.sportsgirl.com.au

US

American Eagle

www.ae.com

Bloomingdale's

www.bloomingdales.com

Charming Charlie

www.charmingcharlie.com

Claire's

www.claires.com

Francesca's

www.francescas.com

Nordstrom

www.nordstrom.com

Von Maur

www.vonmaur.com

GLOBAL

Alexander McQueen

www.alexandermcqueen.com

Anthropologie

www.anthropologie.com

ASOS

www.asos.com

Burberry

www.burberry.com

Chanel

www.chanel.com

Etsy

www.etsy.com

Ferragamo

www.ferragamo.com

H&M

www.hm.com

Hermès

www.hermes.com

Pucci

www.emiliopucci.com

Ted Baker

www.tedbaker.com

Topshop

www.topshop.com

Urban Outfitters

www.urbanoutfitters.com

Zara

www.zara.com